Prepare to Survive

How to Survive in the
Wilderness

by Tim O'Shei

Consultant: Al Siebert, PhD
Author of *The Survivor Personality*

Capstone
press®
Mankato, Minnesota

Edge Books are published by Capstone Press,
151 Good Counsel Drive, P.O. Box 669, Mankato, Minnesota 56002.
www.capstonepress.com

Library of Congress Cataloging-in-Publication Data
O'Shei, Tim.
    How to survive in the wilderness / by Tim O'Shei.
    p. cm. — (Edge books. Prepare to Survive.)
    Includes bibliographical references and index.
    ISBN-13: 978-1-4296-2281-3 (hardcover)
    ISBN-10: 1-4296-2281-4 (hardcover)
    1. Wilderness survival — Juvenile literature. I. Title. II. Series.
GV200.5.O844 2009
613.6'9 — dc22   2008034520

Summary: Describes tips on how to survive in the wilderness.

Editorial Credits
Angie Kaelberer, editor; Veronica Bianchini, designer; Wanda Winch,
    photo researcher; Sarah L. Schuette, photo stylist; Marcy Morin,
    photo shoot scheduler

Photo Credits
Amy Racina, 27
Capstone Press/Gary Sundermeyer, 15 (all); Capstone Press/Karon Dubke, 4–5, 9,
    16, 21, 25
Getty Images Inc./Hawkins Family, 24; Stone/Darrell Gulin, 26
iStockphoto/AVTG, front cover; Brian Palmer, 20; Doug Cannell, 19 (bottom);
    Jozsef Szasz-Fabian, 22 (helicopter)
Peter Arnold/F. Lukasseck, 8
Rod Whigham, 12, 13, 22, 23, 29 (top)
Shutterstock/aga, 14; Chee-Onn Leong, 6, 7; Dario Sablijak, 19 (top); Dr. Morley
    Read, 18 (bottom); Esther Groen, 18 (top); John Bell, 29 (bottom); Lora Liu,
    back cover; Peter Weber, 22–23; Ronnie Howard, 28; Stephen Strathdee, 17;
    Xavier Marchant, 10–11

Table of Contents

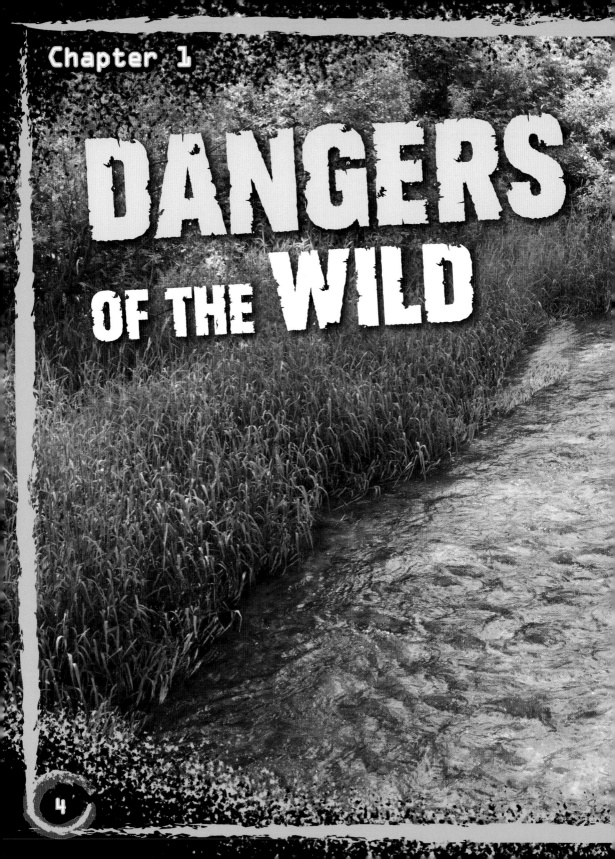

Chapter 1

DANGERS
OF THE WILD

Towering trees cast shade in the sunlight. A gentle breeze rustles the leaves. Rushing rivers and trickling streams create a peaceful hum.

It all seems so pleasant, doesn't it? The wilderness is an attractive place. That's why nature lovers hike, camp, and ski in it.

But the scenery can be misleading. Those trees and rivers can form a maze. Hikers and campers sometimes misread maps. Skiers and snowboarders can take wrong turns. Sometimes airplanes crash into forests. All of these situations lead to one problem — being stuck in the wilderness. What if it happens to you?

The wilderness can be a scary place, especially when you're trying to survive in it. Even in summer, forests can get so chilly that you'll want a blanket. Wind and rain make your body feel even colder. People lost in the wilderness may develop **hypothermia**.

Keeping warm is only part of survival. You also need to find food and water. People can survive for weeks without food. In the wilderness, though, you shouldn't have to go hungry. The wilderness has plenty of food — if you can catch it.

The real problem is water. You need lots of it. Even one day without water can cause **dehydration**. Two or more days without water can be deadly.

While water is a need, too much of it can be a problem. Heavy rains can cause rivers and streams to flood. Rain can also cause dangerous mudslides.

hypothermia – a life-threatening condition that occurs when a person's body temperature falls several degrees below normal

dehydration – a life-threatening medical condition caused by a lack of water

Even if there are no other people around, you're not really alone in the wilderness. The forest is full of animals and insects. Most of them will leave you alone, but some won't, especially if you get in their way. That's where the "wild" comes from in wilderness — so let's learn how to survive.

How to
PACK FOR SURVIVAL

Experienced hikers always carry a backpack or fanny pack filled with survival gear. The tips in this book will help you survive with or without one, but which situation would you rather be in? Include these items:

- first-aid kit
- string or rope
- spoil-free food, such as granola bars and soup or oatmeal packets

- plastic storage bag
- bottles of water
- lighter or matches in a waterproof container

- magnifying glass
- knife or small saw
- compass
- whistle
- collapsible shovel
- blanket
- flashlight
- emergency radio
- cell phone
- global positioning system (GPS) device
- extra batteries
- large, heavy-duty garbage bags

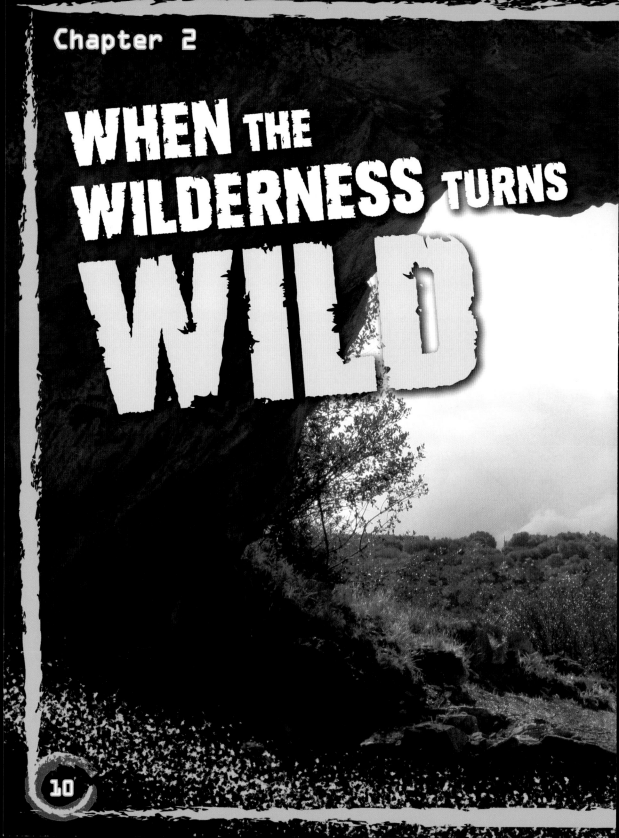

How to

FIND SHELTER

No matter what part of the wilderness you're in, you need shelter. First, look for natural shelter. This can be a cave. It could also be a tangle of downed trees with branches that form a covering.

If you build a shelter, try to find a flat area of land, especially if you're on a mountain or hill. On sloped land, a landslide or **avalanche** could destroy your shelter. Look overhead for anything that could fall on your shelter, like dead tree limbs. Avoid building in the bottom of a valley. Low areas get very cold at night, even in summer.

If you build a shelter near a river, lake, or other waterway, the site should be higher than the water. Otherwise, a heavy rainstorm could send floodwaters your way.

avalanche – a large mass of ice, snow, or earth that suddenly moves down the side of a mountain

SHELTER FROM THE STORM

Most wilderness areas have plenty of natural materials you can use to build a simple shelter. Here's how to build several wilderness shelters:

Lean-to. Find a strong, polelike branch and lean it into a tree. Lean smaller sticks against the pole to form a frame. You also can lean a pole onto a stump, or lean three poles into each other like a tepee.

Use string, rope, or vines to tie the poles together. Then add branches, brush, and leaves for **insulation**. If you have a large garbage bag, you can stretch it between the ground and the tree.

Hut. You'll need long sticks, bendable **reeds**, and string or fishing line. Use the sticks and reeds to make the frame. It can look like a pyramid, a half-circle, or a box. Tie the sticks and reeds together with string or fishing line. Cover the walls with dried leaves, grass, or brush.

insulation – a material that stops heat, sound, or cold from entering or escaping
reed – tall grass with hollow stems
suffocate – to die from lack of oxygen

Body hollow. Dig a hole in the ground about 1 foot (.3 meter) longer and wider than you. The hole should be 18 to 24 inches (46 to 61 centimeters) deep. Crawl in and cover your body with branches and brush. You can also dig a body hollow in the snow. Pile snow on top of the branches for extra insulation.

Snow cave. Find a high snowdrift of firm, packed snow. Dig inward and then upward, so the room is higher than the entrance. This construction will help trap warm air. Make sure you carve a small hole at the top of the cave as a vent. Otherwise, you could **suffocate** from breathing your own carbon dioxide.

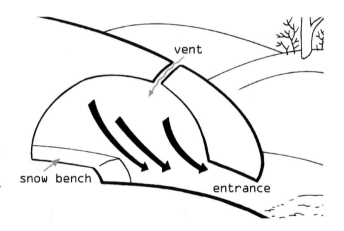

vent

snow bench

entrance

TIP: In a snow cave, carving a snow bench for a bed will keep you slightly warmer than sleeping on the cave floor. Cover the bench with pine needles or branches for more warmth.

How to

MAKE FIRE

Fire provides warmth, cooks food, and boils water. You can live in the wilderness without fire, but your stay will be much more comfortable with it.

First, find a safe spot. Choose an area clear of sticks and branches, low-hanging trees, or anything else that might catch fire accidentally. Lay a circle of large rocks outside the area to contain the fire.

YOU WILL NEED:

tinder - material that lights easily, like dried grass or leaves

kindling - dry sticks and branches that the tinder will catch on fire

fuel - larger logs or coal that will burn a long time

Put the tinder on the ground and lightly lay the kindling over it. Prop your longer sticks and logs over this base by leaning them against one another. Then light the tinder.

tinder

The best way to light a fire is with wooden matches or a lighter. If you don't have either, try:

- Using a magnifying glass or camera lens in the sunlight. If you position it correctly, the lens will focus the sun's rays into a small circle that creates a spark.

kindling

- Creating a spark by striking a piece of flint rock against steel, if you have it. Flint is dark, flat, and breaks easily. Look for flint near a creek.

- Striking two pieces of flint against each other to produce a spark.

fuel

- Rubbing a piece of hard wood against a piece of soft wood or a rock to create a spark.

TIP: Cotton balls covered with petroleum jelly make excellent tinder.

How to

FIND WATER

Food is something your body can live without for a while. Water isn't. If you go more than a couple of days without water, they're almost certain to be the last days of your life.

Luckily, the wilderness usually has ponds, streams, rivers, or lakes. Unluckily, many of them are a drowning hazard. Find a safe place to approach the water. Walk carefully, so you don't fall in.

What if you don't have an easily available source of water? First, avoid activities that make you sweat. Try to do most of your work before sunrise and after sunset.

Second, look for signs that may lead you to water. Animals need water too, so their tracks may lead you to it. If you're in a mountainous area, go downhill. Rivers and streams often run through valleys.

If you still have no luck, wait until dusk and dig a hole that is at least knee-deep. Meanwhile, make a fire and heat some large rocks in it. When your digging hits a moist area of soil, use a stick to knock the hot rocks into the hole. The rocks should make the water in the ground steam upward. Hold a rag or T-shirt overhead to collect the steam. Then suck on the moist fabric. This won't get you much water, but it may be enough to keep you going.

If you have a plastic bag, try tying it around the leaves of a tree branch in the sun. Water should condense off the leaves into the bag.

TIP: If you find snow, make a fire to melt it. Eating snow can cause hypothermia.

How to
FIND FOOD

People can survive several weeks without food. But that doesn't mean you should. Food is fuel for your body. Because you can't exactly order a pizza in the wilderness, you'll have to find food that you might not usually eat.

Here's the first rule of wilderness food: If something moves, it is probably safe to eat. Bugs, rodents, frogs, fish, earthworms — people lost in the wilderness have survived on all of them. But be careful. Some caterpillars, for example, are poisonous. Avoid any brightly colored or hairy insects, as well as those that have a strong odor.

Animals do need some preparation before you can eat them. Remove the wings and legs from bugs. Clean worms in water. Though you can eat most animals raw, it's safer and tastier to cook them — especially the big ones. Remove the feathers, fur, or skin before cooking. Then pull out the entrails, or guts, so that you're left with meat and bones. Boil these parts in a pot or cook them on a rock heated from below by fire.

Many plants are **edible**, but not all. Avoid plants with milky sap. Also steer clear of those with beans, bulbs, or seeds in pods. Don't eat spiny, hairy, or thorny plants. Stay away from plants that have three leaves, like poison ivy. Avoid mushrooms in all cases. Some are edible, but a small number are very poisonous.

TIP: You can test a plant for edibility by separating its leaves, stems, roots, and flowers. Taste one small part of the plant at a time, waiting 8 hours between taste tests. If you feel OK at the end of that time, the plant part is likely safe to eat.

edible – able to be eaten

CROSS A STREAM OR RIVER

Don't cross a stream or river unless you absolutely must. If you do, scout out the best spot. Wide areas tend to be shallower than narrow areas. But remember that wide streams can still be too deep to cross safely.

If you're wading across, grab a strong stick or pole that you can use to stay balanced. Don't remove your shoes. They'll protect your feet from rocks and other hidden hazards. Start slowly, taking one step at a time. Put the pole in front of you to test the area you're about to walk through. If the current seems too strong, or if you find a steep drop-off in the stream floor, go back.

If there is a natural bridge like a fallen log or a series of rocks, step carefully. Logs can fall. Wet rocks are slippery. Be careful and know what's below in case you do fall.

How to

MAKE A TOILET

It's unavoidable — you'll have to relieve yourself. When people are hurt or sick in the wilderness, they may have no other choice but to go in their pants. But if you're able, you should build an outdoor toilet.

Pick a spot at least 100 yards (91 meters) from your shelter. Dig a hole and do what needs to be done. If you have no toilet paper, use leaves, but be careful of poison ivy and other three-leaved plants. Afterward, fill in the hole with dirt. Human waste has a strong scent that attracts flies, rodents, and larger animals.

How to

SEND RESCUE SIGNALS

Send rescue signals from the highest, clearest point possible. Doing this gives rescuers flying overhead in planes or helicopters the best chance to see you.

Some rescue signals that work well:

- Make three fires in a triangle shape.
- Spread a blanket in a clear area. A color that doesn't blend in with the surroundings works best.
- In the dark, use the light from a cell phone, MP3 player, or flashlight to signal aircraft flying overhead.
- In a snowy area, carve a message into the snow, such as "HELP" or "SOS." Fill it in with sticks, brush, and pine needles.
- Make noise. Blow a whistle, bang a stick on a rock, or just plain yell.

Finally, don't travel too far. If you wander too far away from your shelter or from main paths in the woods, it may be hard for rescuers to find you.

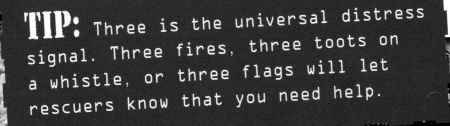

TIP: Three is the universal distress signal. Three fires, three toots on a whistle, or three flags will let rescuers know that you need help.

BRENNAN HAWKINS

Eleven-year-old Brennan Hawkins was on a Boy Scout camping trip in the Uinta Mountains of Utah on June 17, 2005. He took the wrong trail after he was called back to camp for dinner.

For four days, Brennan wandered through the forest. He drank water from streams but was careful not to fall in. He ate wild mint leaves that he found. To keep warm at night, he tucked his legs inside his sweatshirt.

Meanwhile, as many as 3,000 people searched for Brennan. Rescuers found him on June 21.

When asked what he thought about during his ordeal, Brennan said that he was scared that he wouldn't see his family again. That fear likely helped him focus on surviving.

Brennan (center) was cold and hungry when he was found.

USE THE SKY FOR DIRECTIONS

The best way to know directions is to have a compass, which always points north. If you don't have one, you can rely on the sky. The sun rises in the east and sets in the west. At night, look for the bright North Star. It's about halfway between the Big Dipper and Cassiopeia. These **constellations** are visible throughout the year.

How to

WASH YOUR CLOTHES

If you're near a river or stream, wash your clothes and leave them on a rock to dry in the sun. No water? Turn your clothes inside out and let them bake in the sun. But if you're stuck in the cold, you'll probably want to keep your clothes on — dirty or not.

constellation — a group of stars that form a shape

What If

YOU COME ACROSS A BEAR?

Bears don't want to attack humans. As long as we don't put them in a defensive situation, they'll usually leave us alone. Here are some tips:

- Food attracts bears, so do your cooking at least 100 feet (30 meters) from where you sleep. Don't store any food in your shelter. It's best not to even sleep in the same clothes you wore while cooking.

- If you spot a bear, stay as far away as possible. Be especially careful to avoid female bears with cubs.

- Don't try to sneak around a bear. Surprised bears are angry bears! Talk loudly and make sure the bear knows you're there.

- If you do get too close to a bear, stay still. Usually it won't attack. If the bear does attack, curl up and play dead. If the attack continues and you need to fight the bear, hit it in the nose.

AMY RACINA

In 2003, Amy Racina was hiking alone through California's Sierra Nevada Mountains. She slipped and plunged down a 60-foot (18-meter) cliff. Both of her legs were broken. Bones popped out of her bloody right knee.

Luckily, Racina had packed a backpack full of survival gear. She cleaned her knee with hydrogen peroxide. She used a scarf to slow the bleeding. Then Racina pulled out her propane tank and stove. She made chicken soup to warm herself.

Racina could use only her arms to move. For three slow, painful days, she inched toward a trail. Finally, she heard a whistle in the distance. Racina used a knife to cut a hole in the bottom of an empty water jug. She used this homemade megaphone to call for help. It worked! Three hikers found Racina and helped her to safety. Racina's preparation and determination helped her survive.

Jake Van Akkeren (standing) helped rescue Racina (seated).

27

What if

YOU MEET A COUGAR?

If you meet a cougar, don't run. Instead, make yourself seem as big as possible. Hold open your jacket, if you have one, and spread your arms wide. Make loud noises and wave your hands. If the cat does attack, fight back and hit its nose and mouth. Protect your neck and throat. Cougars bite these areas to kill their prey.

What if

YOU MEET A SNAKE?

Stay away! Most snakes don't look at people as their next meal. But they will bite if they feel threatened. They strike fast and from long distances. A coiled-up snake can strike a distance equal to half its body length.

If you are bitten, wash the bite. Keep the wound below your heart. This action should slow the flow of **venom** through your body. Wrap a bandage or cloth 2 to 4 inches (5 to 10 centimeters) above the bite. Try to get medical help as soon as possible.

BE PREPARED!

You now have much of the information you need to survive alone in the wild. But there's one thing you can't pack in a backpack — determination. People who survive in the wilderness are determined to live. This determination helps them make good decisions and stay alive until they are rescued.

venom – poisonous liquid produced by animals such as snakes

Glossary

avalanche (A-vuh-lanch) — a large mass of ice, snow, or earth that suddenly moves down the side of a mountain

constellation (kahn-stuh-LAY-shuhn) — a group of stars that forms a shape

dehydration (dee-hy-DRAY-shuhn) — a life-threatening medical condition caused by a lack of water

edible (ED-uh-buhl) — able to be eaten

hazard (HAZ-urd) — something that is dangerous

hydrogen peroxide (HYE-druh-juhn puh-ROCKS-eyed) — a liquid used to kill germs

hypothermia (hye-puh-THUR-mee-uh) — a life-threatening condition that occurs when a person's body temperature falls several degrees below normal

insulation (in-suh-LAY-shun) — a material that stops heat, sound, or cold from entering or escaping

reed (REED) — tall grass with a hollow stem

suffocate (SUHF-uh-kate) — to die from lack of oxygen

venom (VEN-uhm) — poisonous liquid produced by animals such as snakes

Read More

Norman, Tony. *Survival Skills.* Action Sports. Milwaukee: Gareth Stevens, 2006.

O'Shei, Tim. *Alone in the Wilderness!: Brennan Hawkins' Story of Survival.* True Tales of Survival. Mankato, Minn.: Capstone Press, 2008.

O'Shei, Tim. *The World's Most Amazing Survival Stories.* The World's Top Tens. Mankato, Minn.: Capstone Press, 2007.

Rohr, Ian. *Survival Against the Odds.* Real Deal. Philadelphia: Chelsea House, 2005.

Internet Sites

FactHound offers a safe, fun way to find educator-approved Internet sites related to this book.

Here's what you do:

1. Visit *www.facthound.com*
2. Choose your grade level.
3. Begin your search.

This book's ID number is 9781429622813.

FactHound will fetch the best sites for you!

Index